CW01064674

Original title:
The Truth About Everything

Editor: Theodor Taimla
Author: Paul Pääsuke
ISBN HARDBACK: 978-9916-763-16-2
ISBN PAPERBACK: 978-9916-763-17-9

Mirrors of Certainty

Glimmers reveal what's hidden deep,
Within the heart where secrets keep.
Reflections speak of truths once told,
In mirrors framed with edges gold.

Silent whispers, soft and clear,
Echo bonds that we hold dear.
Paths we've walked, and dreams we've traced,
In mirrored thoughts, our futures faced.

Lost in moments, shadows play,
Mirrors guide our mental stray.
Certainty in shifting light,
Holding firm through darkest night.

In the glass, our selves unfold,
Past and present, futures hold.
Mirrors show us what we seek,
Truth unveiled, no longer meek.

Whispers of Insight

Soft the wind in twilight calls,
Through the leaves as dusk appalls.
Gentle whispers fill the air,
Secrets cherished, moments rare.

In the calm of night's embrace,
Insight hides in quiet space.
Thoughts emerge from silent streams,
Leading paths to woven dreams.

Voices linger, faint and near,
Guiding steps to visions clear.
Through the dark and into light,
Wisdom found in whispers slight.

Subtle hints and gentle sound,
In the air they twirl around.
Truths once veiled, now come to sight,
In the whispers of the night.

Timeless Candor

In the heart of ages past,
Voices echo, strong and vast.
Candor speaks in tones so clear,
Truths that time could never smear.

Moments held in amber light,
Stories told in endless night.
Through the years, the echoes blend,
Timeless words that never end.

Honesty in every tale,
Woven through the stars so pale.
Candor stands against the tide,
Steadfast in its lucid stride.

Lessons learned and wisdom gained,
In the annals truth remains.
Timeless candor, always true,
Guiding light when days are new.

Unvarnished Tales

Raw and honest words unravel,
Through the paths where truth will travel.
Stories bare of gilded flair,
Essence pure, beyond compare.

In the weave of tales we spin,
Honesty lies deep within.
Every verse and every line,
Holds a truth that's genuine.

Through the haze of dreams and lies,
Unvarnished tales in night skies rise.
Against illusion, they stand tall,
Truthful echoes, none shall fall.

In the heart of every lore,
Truth resides at story's core.
Unadorned and purely bright,
Tales that shine with honest light.

Unraveled Mysteries

Beneath the stars, a tale untold,
In whispers soft, the night unfolds.
Beyond the reach of light's embrace,
Lie secrets hidden in void's space.

The moonlight dances on the waves,
Reviving dreams from shadowed caves.
In twilight's hush, the truths appear,
Once lost in darkness, now so near.

Stars align in hidden codes,
Guiding paths on secret roads.
Wisdom found in silent tides,
Unraveled mysteries, the soul's guide.

Decoding the Infinite

In the vast expanse of cosmic mind,
Patterns in the void we find.
Every star, a cryptic sign,
In space and time, our fates entwine.

Numbers dance in silent lore,
Infinity's tale, forevermore.
Echoes of eternity ring,
In the song the cosmos sing.

Celestial maps, a guide so true,
Unveil the paths we journey through.
Decoding the infinite, we strive,
Unlocking truths that long survive.

Hidden Dialogues

In shadows deep, the whispers rise,
Stories told in secret sighs.
Silent voices, hidden well,
In every echo, a truth to tell.

Leaves rustle in a subtle code,
Silent dialogues on nature's road.
In the wind's soft, eerie breath,
Lie words unspoken until death.

The ancient stones, they speak in time,
Of ages past and olden rhyme.
Hidden dialogues, unseen and heard,
In every beat, a secret word.

Unseen Realities

Beyond the veil of human sight,
Lies realms of wonder, pure and bright.
In every atom, worlds collide,
In unseen spaces, they reside.

Dreams reveal the hidden planes,
Where forgotten magic reigns.
In the mirrors of the mind,
Unseen realities we find.

Through the lens of inner eye,
Other realms begin to fly.
Exploring depths of vast unknown,
Where unseen realities are shown.

Stripped Down Life

Like leaves in autumn's cold grasp,
We shed our layers one by one,
Till only truth remains to last,
A bare soul under the sun.

The fleeting robes of earthly care,
Slip away in the moon's glow,
Love and time, simple and rare,
Like rivers they ceaselessly flow.

Embrace the honest, open space,
The canvas of existence pure,
Each moment's undressed grace,
A path to inner allure.

The weight of masks and worldly show,
Removed like shadows in the day,
In naked essence, we come to know,
The stripped down life in elegant sway.

Unobscured Moments

When twilight dances in the night,
And stars unveil their silent tales,
We glimpse the world's hidden might,
Unobscured by mortal veils.

Time's breath whispers through the trees,
A song of days yet to unfold,
With every sigh, the heart it frees,
Moments bright and uncontrolled.

In the hush of dawn's first kiss,
Where dreams and daylight softly blend,
We find a peace in moments bliss,
That need no reason to defend.

Let go of clocks and numbered hours,
Embrace the present, undefined,
In nature's quiet, subtle powers,
Unobscured moments, pure and kind.

Through the Veil

Beyond the mist of waking sight,
Lies realms unseen by mortal eyes,
A world of shadows, faint and light,
Through the veil, the spirit flies.

Whispers from a distant shore,
Echo in the heart's deep well,
Souls that lived and dreamt before,
In mysteries they gently dwell.

Between the known and the unknown,
A curtain thin as moonlit lace,
Waiting for the seeds we've sown,
To bloom in a timeless space.

Through the veil, a softened glow,
Reveals the truths we cannot see,
In every silence, treasures grow,
And set the mind and spirit free.

Secrets of Existence

In the quiet hush of night,
Where whispers weave through star-lit skies,
Existence shares its hidden light,
In secrets told to open eyes.

The heartbeat of the world below,
A rhythm ancient, pure, and deep,
In every grain of sand we know,
Life's mysteries that never sleep.

Within the petals of a rose,
Or in the depths of ocean blue,
The secrets of existence close,
Are waiting for the seeker true.

Deciphering the silent code,
Of nature's ever-turning wheel,
We walk along the sacred road,
And to the earth, our hearts we seal.

Existential Musings

In twilight's tender glow, I ponder deep,
Of cosmic dreams where silent shadows creep.
A fleeting moment caught in time's embrace,
We chase the echoes of an endless race.

Stars above, they whisper ancient tales,
Of love and loss, where human courage fails.
In every breath, we grasp for meaning true,
Beneath the sky's eternal, boundless blue.

The heart beats on, a drum within the night,
Seeking solace in the softest light.
For every step, a question left unsaid,
In life's grand dance, we tread where angels tread.

Through tangled thoughts, the mind's vast wilderness,
We search for truths beyond this earthly mess.
In silence, answers come on wings of dreams,
Illuminating life's mysterious schemes.

The Naked Reality

Stripped of illusions, we stand bare,
In truth's cold light, there's naught to spare.
A mirror shines with unrelenting glare,
Reflecting paths beyond despair.

The mask we wore, now fallen away,
Reveals the scars of night and day.
In vulnerability, we find our say,
A voice that guides in life's array.

No longer shadows, but forms of light,
We navigate through dark and bright.
The simple truths, our guiding sight,
To onward march with hopeful might.

In every heartbeat, raw and true,
We find the courage to renew.
For in the naked, we pursue,
A world reborn, both old and new.

Peeling the Layers

Each layer sheds a tale untold,
Of secrets tight, of dreams grown old.
The skin we wore, a cloak of gold,
Now falls away as truths unfold.

Within, the whispers of the soul,
Unravel tales that make us whole.
A journey deep, where rivers roll,
To find the self, the true, the goal.

Unmasked, the essence pure and bright,
Emerges from the darkest night.
In shadows cast, we find our light,
A soul reborn, a fearless flight.

The journey ends where it began,
Discovering the inner man.
For in each layer, new we plan,
To understand this life, we can.

Burning Through Illusions

In flames of truth, illusions die,
The smoke a veil across the sky.
We see beyond the whispered lie,
To view the world with clearer eye.

The fire dances, fierce and wild,
Consuming thoughts both vain and mild.
In ashes, wisdom once defiled,
A phoenix rises, undefiled.

Through burning light, we face the night,
In courage, fight the blinding fright.
Emerging from the flames, contrite,
A soul renewed, with clearer sight.

Beyond the fire, a world revealed,\nUnseen, unknown,
now unconcealed.
In every ember, wounds are healed,
A truth, unyielding, now our shield.

Naked Revelation

In shadows cast by moonlit skies,
Truths emerge, with no disguise.
Whispers echo, bold and stark,
Illuminating the darkest dark.

Veils of doubt, now lifted high,
Secrets unveiled, no need to pry.
Essence bare, the soul unveiled,
In pure light, all fears have sailed.

Silent nights, with voices clear,
The heart reveals what it holds dear.
Layers shed, a stark rebirth,
Honest moments, of infinite worth.

Masks discarded, lies dissolved,
In this clarity, we're evolved.
Stripped of pretense, we now stand,
Naked truth, the promised land.

Stories Uncloaked

In ancient tales, the past resides,
With every echo, history confides.
Unseen threads, the seams of time,
Untold stories, pure and prime.

Books unopened, gather dust,
Yet within, legends thrust.
Words unfurl, in silent scream,
Narratives born from endless dream.

Timeless whispers, journeys old,
Names and faces, truths retold.
Fables sing of love and pain,
In each recount, lives sustain.

Uncloaked stories, free to roam,
Hearts of the lost find their home.
In every verse, the essence stirs,
Lives intersect through ancient words.

Unfolding Verities

Petals of truth, just starting to bloom,
Mysteries unveiled, dispelling gloom.
Layer by layer, unveiled bliss,
Knowledge comes with every kiss.

In silent moments, wisdom starts,
Bringing light to shadowed parts.
Glimpses of a greater scheme,
Truths unfold in a lucid dream.

Threads of life, once tightly bound,
Now unwind, as truths are found.
Verities rise, clear and bright,
Guiding souls through endless night.

In each breath, a new truth grows,
Clarity through life's ebbs and flows.
Maps of the soul, laid bare to see,
Unfolding truths, eternally.

Cipher of Existence

In cosmic code, our fates entwine,
Cryptic paths, the stars design.
Life's enigma, vast and deep,
Within its cipher, secrets keep.

Patterns dance in celestial script,
Whispers from the astral crypt.
Clues dispersed in night's serene,
Unraveling the in-between.

Existence scripts in silent rhyme,
Words transcending space and time.
Every heartbeat, every sigh,
Decoding truths that never die.

Mystery's essence, woven tight,
In shadows dark and starlit light.
Each revelation brings us near,
To the cipher of existence, clear.

Untold Narratives

In shadows linger stories deep,
Where unseen whispers softly creep.
Silence holds what tongues forsake,
Mysteries for the curious to sake.

A tapestry of dreams awaits,
Woven tight by hidden fates.
Eyes that dare to pierce the veil,
Unlock tales where secrets sail.

In the twilight of the mind,
Forgotten echoes you will find.
Truth and myth entwine as one,
Tales untold by setting sun.

In the mirror's quiet gaze,
Worlds unspoken start to blaze.
As hearts reveal what lips withhold,
Narratives in darkness told.

Through the mists of yesteryears,
Journey back with unshed tears.
Unveil the past in hushed descent,
Untold stories, whispered scent.

Perceptive Realities

Beyond the eyes, the soul does see,
A world unseen by you and me.
Truths not bound by earthly plane,
In silent realms, unfelt, remain.

Perception shapes the world we seek,
In strength, the quiet and the meek.
Different eyes, a thousand tales,
Each one veiling different wails.

Colors blend where thoughts collide,
Reality from heart divide.
Shadows dance where secrets peek,
Wisdom found by those who seek.

Time's illusion we forget,
Moments lost in love's vignette.
Every heartbeat holds a view,
Of realities anew.

Gaze within and softly feel,
Realms where dreams and fears are real.
Perception's key unlocks the gates,
To worlds unseen, where magic waits.

Core Impressions

Deep within where heartbeats sing,
Lie impressions, truth does cling.
In every pulse, a story tells,
Of joys, of sorrows, hidden wells.

The core of self, a mystic flame,
Burns with love, with grief, with name.
Each impression scars and mends,
A tale begun that never ends.

In laughter's light and tear's embrace,
Life's core impressions interlace.
Through storm and peace, our souls we weave,
In moments fond, in times we grieve.

Impressions etched like ancient scrolls,
On hearts and minds, like age-old tolls.
They guide us through our wandering days,
In shadows deep, in sunlit rays.

In quiet times, reflections speak,
Of journeys hard, of paths unique.
Core impressions, essence true,
Shape the old and birth the new.

Seeing with Heart

Eyes alone can't capture light,
Soul must peer beyond the sight.
Through the heart, true vision's found,
In symphonies of life's surround.

Feel the whispers in the breeze,
Comfort found in ancient trees.
With heart, perceive what love reveals,
Truth in silence, wound that heals.

Glimpse the world in hues of grace,
See the smiles on every face.
Empathy's embrace so near,
With heart's gaze, the world comes clear.

Tend the fire of inner sight,
In the stillness of the night.
Heartfelt vision never lies,
In its glow, pure beauty lies.

Craft each moment with a start,
Seeing all with open heart.
Life's true essence softly leans,
In the landscapes of our dreams.

Beyond the Surface

Beneath the waves of silent seas,
Where dreams converge and worries cease.
Mysteries swirl in unseen grace,
Hidden truths in watery space.

The depths conceal untold lore,
Awaiting those who seek for more.
In shadows dark, the light is found,
Whispers soft in sea's surround.

Glimmers shine in twilight's sweep,
Secrets guard a mystic keep.
Past the veil where mermaids tread,
Ancient tales in silence spread.

Seek the marvels not yet seen,
Delve where silent passages lean.
In waters cool and shadows lean,
Lies the soul of ocean's dream.

Illusions Demystified

Shadows dance in moonlit glade,
Veils of mist in night's cascade.
Flickers faint, a hesitant glow,
Revealing worlds we scarcely know.

Mirrors bend reality's gait,
Warping truth at every rate.
Through the glass, both bright and dim,
Lies the path to sights most grim.

Gazes lost in smoky haze,
Mystic symbols fill the maze.
Truths emerge in cryptic form,
Mystery turns in endless storm.

Unveil the masks that cloaks shall bear,
For in the depths, all truths lay bare.
Conundrums fold and secrets break,
Illusions fall in moonlight's wake.

Exposed Mysteries

Veils once thick with secrets held,
Now reveal where whispers dwelled.
Truths emerge from shadows deep,
Hidden paths where dreams once sleep.

In shadows cast by moonlight's touch,
Mysteries long we dared not clutch.
Eclipsed by night, yet bright as day,
Veiled enigmas fade away.

Forgotten tales, once cloaked in dark,
Now shine with truth's resplendent spark.
In ancient lore, the woven thread,
Of hidden secrets, softly spread.

What once was cloaked in veils so grand,
Now lies revealed in glowing hand.
Unshaded by the shadows past,
Exposed mysteries here at last.

Fundamental Insights

Beneath the layers of lore and myth,
The core of truth lies clear and swift.
Foundations firm, in wisdom's flight,
Revealing all with pure insight.

In questions deep and answers wise,
The essence of the mind does rise.
Beyond the surface, clear and bright,
Lies nature's secret, sharp as light.

The essence of the earth and sky,
In every star and leaf nearby.
Grasp the threads of nature's weave,
In solid ground, belief conceive.

Through simple truths and clear accords,
The universe its secrets hoards.
Fundamental, clear as day,
Wisdom shines, it lights the way.

Veiled Transparencies

In whispers roam the veils of light,
Unseen threads of day and night,
Ephemeral, yet standing clear,
The silent truths we hold so near.

Between the shadow and the gleam,
Lie the whispers of a dream,
Veiled words that softly dance,
Invisible in their expanse.

In translucent sheets of time,
Lie the secrets so sublime,
Unfolding with a gentle sigh,
As moonlight whispers from the sky.

Curtains drawn by unseen hands,
Of translucent shifting sands,
Hold the secrets, pure and free,
In veiled transparencies, we see.

Secrets Unraveled

Underneath the moon's soft glow,
Where whispered winds in silence flow,
Lies a world where secrets dwell,
Stories only time can tell.

A tapestry of hidden threads,
Woven where the daylight treads,
Each unravelled strand reveals,
Truths that morning light conceals.

In the shadows, shadows play,
Revealing secrets, night to day,
Untold tales of love and grief,
Woven in each fallen leaf.

With courage, let their bindings free,
Secrets waiting patiently,
Truth shall rise from darkened streams,
To dance within our waking dreams.

Clarity in Chaos

In the storm where shadows meet,
Where time and tide in turmoil greet,
Amid chaos, clear and bright,
Emerges truth from out of sight.

Tangled paths of winding sound,
Where order seldom can be found,
In the noise and wild embrace,
A crystal vision finds its place.

Chaos masks the hidden core,
Where clarity begins to soar,
Amidst the tumult, there stands light,
To guide us through the darkest night.

Within the storm, a silent voice,
Whispering of choice and choice,
In the madness, truth takes seed,
Clarity in chaos, we need.

Unvarnished Insights

In simplicity lies the key,
Truth unvarnished we can see,
Beyond the masks and veils we wear,
Unveil insights bold and fair.

Raw and honest, free from shines,
Gleam the depths in simple lines,
Bare the soul and let it breathe,
In the truths that lies beneath.

With courage pierce the hidden shroud,
Soft and gentle, not too loud,
Whispers of pure honesty,
In unvarnished clarity.

Step into the light so pure,
With unguarded heart and sure,
Keen insights we shall gain,
In unvarnished truth remain.

Truth Unveiled

In the quiet hush of dawn,
Where secrets lie, and truths are drawn,
The heart unburdens, free from shade,
In light, all shadows start to fade.

Whispered winds through ancient trees,
Reveal the stories on the breeze,
Each leaf a testament to time,
Each whisper speaks in silent rhyme.

Underneath the starlit shroud,
The soul stands naked, strong, and proud,
No more masks, just who we are,
In truth's embrace, we've come so far.

The moon reflects our inner light,
Each hidden fear, a starry sight,
In clarity, our spirits heal,
For only truth can wounds reveal.

As night's veil is gently torn,
A new, untainted day is born,
In honesty, we're unafraid,
In truthful dawn, we're unbetrayed.

Intrinsic Exposures

Within the layers of our soul,
Where inner thoughts and dreams unroll,
Lies a mirror, pure and bright,
Reflecting truths in silent light.

Beneath the surface, more to see,
Than outward glances may decree,
Each hidden depth, a world unveiled,
A silent journey through the veiled.

In shadows cast by mind's own eye,
Where fears and hopes and wishes lie,
Embracing all, yet holding tight,
To truths that guide us through the night.

In moments still, our core exposed,
When all the world is juxtaposed,
We find the strength to just be real,
In authenticity, we heal.

The beauty of the unadorned,
Pure essence, not by judgment scorned,
In self-acceptance, we find grace,
And face the world with naked face.

Crystal Clear Echoes

Echoes in the morning mist,
Truths revealed by sunlight's kiss,
Clear as glass, the echoes ring,
Through the mountains, hearts and spring.

Whispers of a crystal stream,
Speaking softly in a dream,
Each droplet tells a story rare,
Of honesty laid pure and bare.

In the silence of the night,
Echoes dance in silver light,
Words unspoken, yet so loud,
In their truth, we are avowed.

Luminous reflections clear,
Dispelling every doubt and fear,
In the mirror of the soul,
Truths like echoes, make us whole.

As the sun begins to rise,
Reflected in the morning skies,
Crystal echoes of the past,
Guide us to our truth at last.

No Masks Allowed

Take off the masks we wear each day,
Let truths shine through, come what may,
In the mirror of our soul,
Only raw and pure, we're whole.

In the stillness of the dawn,
The masquerade forever gone,
Lift the veil and let hearts see,
In bare beauty, wild and free.

Unmask the fears, the hidden pain,
Let the skies pour cleansing rain,
In the naked light of truth,
We reclaim our spirit's youth.

No facade to hide behind,
Open heart, and open mind,
In the realm where masks are shunned,
Find the courage to be one.

With vulnerability in tow,
Our true essence starts to flow,
In the light of what's revealed,
Wounds of yesteryear are healed.

Veils Lifted

In twilight's gentle, fleeting grace,
A dance of shadows, light's embrace.
Whispers of truths in evening's kiss,
Unraveled secrets, endless abyss.

Eyes that see beyond the night,
Reveal the hidden, purest light.
Fears dissolve in dawn's sweet gleam,
Dreams awaken, as veils redeem.

The heart, a mirror, clear and bright,
Reflects the soul's unguarded flight.
Masks are shed with each new breath,
Life reborn from shadowed death.

Veils are lifted, pure and clear,
Truths uncovered, without fear.
The world unfolds in colors true,
A spectrum vast, forever new.

In every lifted veil, a chance,
To see life's intricate, sacred dance.
Mysteries unveiled, tales untwist,
In the clarity of dawn's soft mist.

Echoes of Honesty

A voice that trembles not with fear,
Speaks truth in tones so crystal clear.
Echoes of honesty resound,
In hearts where sincerities are found.

Eyes that meet in candid gaze,
Reflect the truth in sunlit haze.
No shadows shade the earnest plea,
Trust is born where truth is free.

Words aligned in flawless grace,
Unveil the soul, the heart's own space.
Promises are kept in sight,
Dreams endure through darkest night.

In stillness of the open heart,
Truth and love shall never part.
Faith in honesty, a beacon's light,
Guides us through the thickening night.

Echoes of a truth sets free,
A world unchained, in honesty.
The dawn emerges, purest hue,
In the light of what is true.

Shattered Illusions

A glass of lies, so finely spun,
Shatters in the rising sun.
Fragments glint in morning's breath,
Illusions fade, reveal what's left.

Eyes that hope, now see so clear,
Truth emerges, conquers fear.
Whispers morph to clarion calls,
Through the echoed, shattered walls.

Dreams once built on fragile sand,
Lie broken by a firmer hand.
Yet wisdom grows from fractured tales,
Strength reborn from each betrayal.

In every shard, a lesson learned,
Truth in pain, eternally earned.
From illusion's grave, new life emerges,
In the darkness, light converges.

Shattered illusions pave the way,
For brighter truths in light of day.
As the mirrors crash and bleed,
New reflections are decreed.

Naked Verities

In a world of woven lies,
Where the veils of pretense rise.
Truth stands bare, in stark release,
Naked verities bring peace.

Eyes unclouded, see the core,
Stripped of falseness, we explore.
Layers peel, reveal the frame,
Unveiling truths that have no name.

In naked verities, we find,
Clarity of heart and mind.
Love unfeigned, and friendships true,
Amidst the skies of azure blue.

The winds of truth, so pure and clear,
Sweep away the dust of fear.
In the raw and tender soul,
Naked verities console.

Through the world's most intricate lies,
Truth ascends and never dies.
In the bare, unguarded light,
We find our way, our sight, our right.

Depths of Awareness

In shadows deep, where thoughts do swim,
A silent realm, beyond the rim.
Whispers of truth, in silence weave,
A tapestry minds perceive.

Beneath the waves of conscious streams,
Lie hidden realms, within our dreams.
Echoes of wisdom, softly they call,
Guiding us through the veils that fall.

An ocean vast, of inner sight,
Awakened by the quiet night.
Seeking the depths, where secrets sleep,
In the stillness, meanings seep.

By lanterns dim, we chart the course,
Through realms of thought, a gentle force.
Each revelation, a subtle hue,
Painting the skies of insight's view.

Awareness blooms, like morning light,
Dispelling shadows, piercing night.
Through every glance, and breath we take,
We find the soul, awake, awake.

Symphony of Realities

From cosmos vast, where stars align,
A symphony, where realms entwine.
Notes of existence, hum and sigh,
In every breath, a world nearby.

Melody of time, in endless flight,
Weaves through the day, and through the night.
Each moment sings its unique song,
In harmony, we all belong.

Beyond the veil of space and thought,
Echoing truths, eternally sought.
A chorus grand, of life's embrace,
Mutual rhythm, in every place.

Infinite verses, hearts compose,
In subtle dance, reality flows.
Strings of fate, and winds of change,
Create the symphony, vast and strange.

In silent woods, or bustling streets,
The music of the universe beats.
We are the notes, the grand refrain,
Eternal song, through joy and pain.

Pure Exposition

In words profound, hearts do confess,
Emotions raw, no need for dress.
Every syllable, a soul laid bare,
In purest form, beyond compare.

Through written lines, thoughts are unveiled,
Truths once hidden, now regaled.
In letters shaped, and pages turned,
Passions ignited, knowledge burned.

A canvas white, with ink's embrace,
Reveals the mind, its secret place.
Each mark upon its pristine face,
A testament to life's own grace.

As poets pen, and authors write,
They cast a beacon in the night.
Exposing worlds, both dark and bright,
Within the reader, sparks ignite.

In exposition, pure and clear,
We find connections, near and dear.
Through every tale, and verse expressed,
Our shared humanity's confessed.

Illuminated Veils

Veils of shadow, softly fall,
Concealing truths, known to all.
But light breaks through, in slanted beams,
Illuminating silent dreams.

The curtains drawn, reveal the glow,
Of hidden realms, that few may know.
In twilight's hush, where whispers creep,
Enlightenment, begins to seep.

Each beam of light, a secret shares,
Of ancient love, and silent prayers.
In every shadow, truth does hide,
Awaiting dawn, to be our guide.

The veils they lift, in morning's grace,
Revealing life, its sacred place.
Through luminous paths, we tread with care,
Finding wisdom, everywhere.

In light and dark, a dance it weaves,
A fabric of the soul believes.
Through veils once dim, now clear and bright,
We journey forth, to endless light.

Raw Perceptions

In shadows cast, where whispers lie,
A world unseen by naked eye.
Truths emerge from hidden views,
Revealing depths in varied hues.

Moments blend in twilight's grace,
Echoes drift through time and space.
Each sensation, sharp and clear,
Forms a path for us to steer.

Patterns dance in streams of thought,
We chase fragments cosmos brought.
In the raw, perceptions bloom,
Balancing on edge of gloom.

Unfolding leaves of memory,
Turn the page, set essence free.
In silence, find the subtle rhyme,
Mark the beats with passing time.

Feel the pulse in every breath,
Knowledge gained in life's bequest.
Infinite the sights we'll see,
Raw perceptions, destiny.

Crystalline Perspectives

Through prisms fine, we gaze anew,
Shattered light refracts our view.
Glimmers of a clearer thought,
Found in fractals finely wrought.

Nature's art in frozen time,
Etched in crystal, pure, sublime.
Each reflection casts a tale,
In its depths, the past unveiled.

Paused in moments, still and bright,
Patterns form in threads of light.
Clarity in fractured beams,
Ties together fleeting dreams.

Facets turn, revealing more,
Crystalline perspectives soar.
In these angles, truths align,
Connecting hearts through space and time.

Dive within the crystal's core,
Find the essence, and explore.
Infinite the clarity,
Crystalline, our sanity.

Pillars of Clarity

In seeking truth, we find our stance,
Pillars rise through circumstance.
Structures built on clear intent,
Hold the weight of souls unbent.

Foundations firm in morning light,
Shadows cast by dawn's first sight.
On these stones, our paths we lay,
Guided through the vast array.

Winds may shift, and tides may flow,
Yet in clarity, we grow.
Standing tall through storm and gale,
Strength in truth, we shall prevail.

Each pillar etched with lessons learned,
Moments lived and bridges burned.
In their lines, we trace our past,
Building futures vast and vast.

Guided by the stars above,
Anchored by the ties of love.
Pillars high, in clarity,
Mark the way for you and me.

Truths Entwined

In threads of life, truths intertwined,
Tangled webs in hearts confined.
Stories weave in silken strands,
Binding souls with unseen hands.

Each a tale of joy and pain,
Sunlight breaks through gentle rain.
In the tapestry they form,
Warmth of love and cold of storm.

Hidden knots reveal their place,
Patterns found in woven grace.
Truths entwined in endless flow,
As we dance where rivers go.

Threads of gold and strands of grey,
Form the paths we walk each day.
In their weave, the essence stays,
Guiding us through life's displays.

Embrace the weave, the truths align,
In these bonds, our lives define.
Truths entwined, we find our road,
In the tapestry bestowed.

Absolute Verities

Beneath the moon's steady glow,
The truths of ages softly flow,
Whispering winds through the night,
Their secrets held in silent flight.

Stars that shine with ancient light,
Eons pass within their sight,
Eternal laws govern the dance,
Of time and space and happenstance.

Mountains rise and oceans swell,
Stories of the Earth they tell,
Through the passage of the years,
Their silent witness calms our fears.

In the heart, the truth resides,
Regardless how the world divides,
Unseen threads that bind our fate,
In this cosmic, grand debate.

Timeless is the verity,
In the universe's vast clarity,
With eyes and minds wide to see,
We grasp at our reality.

Hidden in Plain Sight

In the shadow of the day,
Where the mundane hides away,
Mysteries of the world we see,
Cloaked within simplicity.

Clouds that drift in azure blue,
Hold secrets as they do,
Patterns cast in leaf and bark,
Reveal the hidden, small and stark.

Footsteps tread on ancient stone,
Passing stories never known,
In the echo, meant to stay,
Lies the whisper led astray.

Eyes that meet in crowded halls,
Silent answers to the calls,
Lost in ordinary light,
Truth resides in open sight.

Awake we must to what is near,
The signs that speak in silence clear,
For in the plain and common ground,
The profound is always found.

Revelation Depths

Beneath the waves of conscious thought,
Lie secrets we have long sought,
Depths where light has seldom graced,
Wisdom waits in silent space.

Dreams reveal their hidden core,
Truths we've never known before,
Threading through the fabric tight,
Of endless, starry night.

Voices from the depths resound,
Mysteries through time unbound,
In the darkness, light abides,
Revelations none can hide.

Silent echoes, whispered clear,
Lingering close, yet seeming near,
Eternal truths we cannot flee,
Marked by fate for us to see.

Within the quiet of our hearts,
The deepest revelation starts,
In the depths, profound and vast,
We find the future and the past.

Horizons of Reality

Far ahead where sky meets land,
Horizons form a mystic band,
Stretching further than we see,
They hold the key to what will be.

Sunrise paints them every day,
In golden light, a bright array,
Promise of what yet might come,
Songs of hope that we will hum.

Beyond the line where visions rest,
Lies the truth to every quest,
Hidden worlds that wait to show,
The wonders we can never know.

Chasing shadows, chasing dreams,
Life is more than what it seems,
Reality in layers spun,
In the horizon's rising sun.

Infinite the paths we tread,
Horizons stretch in bounds ahead,
In the journey are we freed,
To find the truth in every need.

Veil of Authenticity

In twilight's gleam where truth does hide,
A veil of mist obscures the way.
Yet hearts can feel what eyes deny,
The genuine in shadows play.

Beneath the shroud of pretense placed,
A pulse of life, sincere, beats clear.
Unseen by most, yet felt by all,
Authenticity draws us near.

A whispered truth within the night,
Echoes through the souls who heed.
A call to strip the falsehoods bare,
And plant the seeds of honest deeds.

In mirrors of our daily guise,
Reflections often lie to please.
But in the silence, in ourselves,
The truest forms can find release.

So lift the veil, and breathe the light,
For in the raw, we find our grace.
In authenticity's embrace,
We stand unburdened, free in place.

Shadows Unveiled

Beneath the moon's soft, silver gaze,
The shadows dance in silent lore.
Secrets whispered through the haze,
Of truths that we cannot ignore.

In every darkened corner lies,
A story hidden from the day.
Unspoken words and unseen ties,
In shadow's realm they gently sway.

A flicker here, a glimpse of past,
In shadows' depths, the secrets cast.
They stitch the night with threads of gloom,
Yet hold the dawn within their grasp.

The twilight fades, and darkness stays,
Revealing what the light conceals.
In shadows' embrace, the soul displays,
The truest form that silence feels.

Embrace the night, the quiet tales,
For shadows often light our way.
Unveil the truths behind the veils,
And greet the dawn with no dismay.

Beneath the Façade

A smile painted with careful grace,
Yet hides the storms that rage within.
Faces masked in silent lace,
Conceal the battles yet to win.

Bright laughter rings, a hollow sound,
Echoes deep where fears reside.
In every glance, a secret found,
Beneath the façade, we often hide.

Through mirrored halls of thoughts suppressed,
We wander lost, in dreams confined.
Yet in the heart's untamed recess,
The courage to be real, we find.

Layers thick and walls so high,
Constructed by the fears we face.
Yet love and truth can amplify,
The whispers calling for embrace.

So strip away the masks we wear,
And let the genuine be seen.
For in the raw, the soul laid bare,
We find where true connections glean.

Layers of Reality

Peel the layers, one by one,
Unraveling truths that light denies.
In every fold, a secret spun,
In hidden depths, reality lies.

A fragile thread that ties the seams,
Of life's complex, intricate weave.
In dreams we dream, in hopes it gleams,
The essence of what we believe.

Behind the masks of day and night,
A thousand faces, stories told.
In shadows cast by dawn's first light,
New facets of ourselves unfold.

Layered truths and stacked deceits,
Build the world in which we dwell.
Yet through the cracks, the honest beats,
A rhythm known, a Silent Bell.

So strip the layers thick and deep,
Reveal the soul, unarmed and free.
For in the raw, our hearts do keep,
The purest form of reality.

Hidden Chronicles

In shadows deep, where secrets lie,
Whispers dance, and echoes sigh.
Within the walls of time's embrace,
Unfolding tales in quiet space.

Books of old, with pages worn,
Guarded truths, and legends born.
Silent keepers of the past,
Echoes lingering, shadows cast.

Ancient runes on stones inscribed,
Speak of kingdoms, once revived.
Beneath the stars, an ancient lore,
Whispers secrets, ever more.

Hidden paths where footsteps tread,
Mystic whispers, stories spread.
Unseen forces, softly call,
Chronicling truths, they enthrall.

In the quiet, find the key,
Unlocking mysteries, let them be.
Journey deep into the night,
Where chronicles of old, take flight.

Unmasking Lies

Behind the smiles, a web is spun,
Deceitful words, from lips begun.
Truth obscured by veils so thin,
Masked intentions, seep within.

Eyes that glisten, souls concealed,
In masquerade, their hearts revealed.
Unraveling threads, where shadows lie,
Deceptions melt, beneath the sky.

Beneath the guise, the truth will rise,
In darkness seen, through clearer eyes.
Lies once gilded, now laid bare,
In light of dawn, the truth declare.

Whispers fade, as masks dissolve,
Through silent night, the heart resolves.
Unspoken truths, come to the fore,
Unmasking lies, forevermore.

In clarity the path is shown,
Facing truths once left unknown.
Beyond the shadows, light is found,
Unmasking lies, where hearts are bound.

Fractured Facades

In glistening shards of broken dreams,
Reflections hide, amid the seams.
Exterior smooth, a flawless guise,
Beneath the cracks, the truth belies.

Masks that crumble, slowly fade,
Revealing souls in light and shade.
Facade once firm, begins to peel,
Unveiling scars that time conceal.

Through fractures see the tender light,
A soul laid bare, in truth's pure sight.
No longer hidden, flaws exposed,
In vulnerability, hearts composed.

Piece by piece, the facade breaks,
Revealing depths that time forsakes.
From shattered past, a new emerges,
Through brokenness, the spirit surges.

In fractured lines, a tale is told,
Of broken hearts, and souls consoled.
Beyond the surface, truth will reign,
In fractures deep, new strength is gained.

The Core of Life

Beneath the layers, vast and deep,
The essence of our lives we keep.
In quiet moments, hearts reveal,
The core of life, where truths are real.

Amid the chaos, find the calm,
A quiet soul, a soothing balm.
Through storms and strife, in darkness bright,
The core of life, a guiding light.

In whispered wind, and gentle song,
The heart's true path, it leads us on.
To places where the spirit thrives,
In core of life, our essence strives.

Embrace the depth, the silent pull,
Where life's true meaning, finds its lull.
In heartbeats strong, and breath so pure,
The core of life, let it endure.

With every step, and every breath,
We journey through, from birth to death.
Hold close the truths, through joy or strife,
For in the core, we find our life.

Unveiling Continuum

In whispers of the morning dew,
The world awakes to shades of blue,
A narrative the stars endue,
To guide us where the dreams pursue.

Mountains stretch and rivers wind,
Timeless tales by nature signed,
Through the ages, trails aligned,
In unity, the paths we find.

Cosmic dance of endless skies,
Mysteries where wonder lies,
In every breath, new hope replies,
A journey where the spirit flies.

Waves that kiss the sandy shore,
Echoes from a distant lore,
Histories we can't ignore,
Eternal circles evermore.

Stardust to the earth returns,
Life's eternal wheel that churns,
In this grand design, one learns,
To cherish how the essence burns.

Essence Unfurled

Petals soft in dawn's embrace,
Gentle as a lover's grace,
Trailing dreams in endless chase,
In nature's heart, we find our place.

Skyward birds with song declare,
Moments fleeting, light as air,
A tapestry of hues so rare,
Unfolding stories everywhere.

Ripples in a quiet pond,
Silent bonds that grow beyond,
In reflection, hearts respond,
To the whispered cosmic bond.

Moonbeams on a tranquil night,
Whisper truths with soft delight,
In darkness, seek and find the light,
A dance between the wrong and right.

Steps mindful on earth we tread,
Paths of wisdom, brightly fed,
With every dawn, new chapters read,
Life's essence unfurled, love widespread.

Mindful Realities

Crimson dawn and twilight's hue,
Blend the old with crisply new,
In each breath, a journey's cue,
Reality in mindful view.

Silent whispers of the leaves,
Ancient wisdom each receives,
Through the web that nature weaves,
Harmony the mind perceives.

Ripening fields and rivers flow,
Secrets in their silent show,
Each moment teaching us to know,
The depth within, the seeds we sow.

Through the storms and gentle rain,
Echoes of the heart's refrain,
In stillness, truth is found again,
Undulating peace, a mindful gain.

Paths once wandered, lessons clear,
Journey's worth in every tear,
In the now, discard the fear,
Bound to all that minds revere.

Heartfelt Confessions

In quiet realms, our spirits blend,
Where broken hearts have time to mend,
Whispers flow where thoughts transcend,
A universe our souls defend.

With tender hands, we shape our fate,
Through paths unknown and love innate,
In shadows cast, our hearts relate,
Connecting lives, no broken gate.

Through teardrops in the stormy night,
A hopeful dawn ignites the light,
Confessions spoken with contrite,
Unveiling truths to make things right.

In the dance of hearts sincere,
Soft confessions, free of fear,
A universe brought close and near,
In empathy, the truth we hear.

Love's narrative, a woven thread,
Through words unsaid and tears we've shed,
A bond that lives though worlds have bled,
Heartfelt paths where souls are led.

Seeing Through Shadows

In twilight's gentle, dim embrace,
Where shadows dance and memories trace,
The silent whispers softly sound,
Through darkness, light can still be found.

A flicker in the evening's veil,
Beyond the dusk, where spirits sail,
The heart perceives what eyes may miss,
A world in shadows, full of bliss.

Each silhouette, a secret keeps,
Beneath the stars, where silence weeps,
In every shadow, dreams reside,
Emerging when the fears subside.

The moonlight carves a path anew,
In darkness, a different hue,
Through shaded realms, our souls commune,
With shadows gone, the heart attunes.

As dawn arrives and night recedes,
Enlightened by our shadowed deeds,
Through every dusk, a promise grows,
The light within, forever glows.

The Veil Vanished

A curtain falls, the veil is torn,
From hidden depths, new life is born,
The mysteries once cloaked in night,
Now bask in dawn's forgiving light.

In silence, whispers find their voice,
Beyond the veil, they dare rejoice,
The secrets held, now freely told,
In light, their beauty does unfold.

The veil, a shroud of fear and doubt,
Once held within, now cast about,
With clarity, our visions clear,
We dance in truths that once were near.

Through unveiled eyes, the world is seen,
A tapestry of what has been,
With wisdom gained from shadows past,
The future shines, forever vast.

The veil, no more a binding thread,
In its absence, fears are shed,
With unveiled hearts, we greet the day,
The path ahead, a radiant way.

Foundational Layers

Beneath the surface, depth profound,
Where roots of dreams are tightly wound,
The layers forged through time and care,
Foundations built on faith and dare.

Each stratum tells a tale anew,
Of trials faced and visions true,
Through layers deep, our essence flows,
In every fold, our spirit grows.

From bedrock firm, our hope ascends,
With every layer, strength it lends,
The core beneath, a guiding star,
Defines the path of who we are.

In every layer, wisdom sleeps,
A legacy our spirit keeps,
Through time's embrace, we grow and learn,
From each foundation, we discern.

With every step, we peel away,
The layers of our yesterdays,
Unveiling truths, we rise and see,
The core within, forever free.

Transparent Dreams

In realms of thought where whispers meet,
Transparent dreams, so pure, discreet,
They float on winds of silent night,
Illuminating hearts so bright.

Through veils unseen, these dreams emerge,
On waves of hope, their truths converge,
Invisible to naked eyes,
Yet clear within where wisdom lies.

These dreams, ethereal and clear,
Reflect the soul's unspoken cheer,
They guide us through the darkest hours,
With promises of latent powers.

In moonlit nights, they softly gleam,
Revealing paths where shadows seem,
To fade away, relinquish hold,
Transparent dreams, so proud and bold.

With each transparent dream we weave,
Our hearts receive, our spirits cleave,
To visions pure, to hopes unseen,
In every dream, a world serene.

Mirage to Matter

Shapes shimmer in the desert air,
Whispers of what could be there.
From ethereal dreams, they scatter,
Turning mirage into matter.

In the heat of distant sand,
Visions dance and shift like sand.
Hope and truth entwine and flatter,
Transforming mirage into matter.

Sunlight glistens, bends and breaks,
Reality flows and forms its stakes.
Dreams and truth weave a strong tether,
Binding mirage into matter.

Oasis blooms with life unseen,
Promises paint a verdant sheen.
Desires sculpt a world much better,
Crafting mirage into matter.

Across the dunes, horizons gleam,
A bridge appears within the dream.
Waking worlds embrace each other,
Blending mirage into matter.

Essence in Focus

Through the lens, the world aligns,
Chaos settles, truth refines.
Each moment sharpens, clear and pure,
Essence in focus, vision sure.

Lights caress the contours bright,
Framing fragments, catching light.
Wisdom glimmers, shadows cure,
Essence in focus, thoughts endure.

Crystalized in perfect frame,
Fleeting whispers call by name.
Clarity's gift, silent and pure,
Essence in focus, paths ensure.

Time distilled in one brief flash,
Memories saved from time's harsh clash.
Eternal truths, moments secure,
Essence in focus, hearts assure.

Capturing life's elusive grace,
Immortalizing time and space.
In each still, hopes reconfigure,
Essence in focus, dreams procure.

Shattered Illusions

Mirrors crack and shadows leap,
Promises break, hearts then weep.
Truths once hidden now arise,
From shattered illusions, one more tries.

Facades crumble, masks give way,
Honesty in light of day.
From dark depths, old habits die,
Through shattered illusions, we can fly.

Veils of deception torn apart,
Exposing truths that shape the heart.
New paths found as lies belie,
From shattered illusions, spirits cry.

Fragments glisten in the night,
Glimmers of hope, a new sight.
Rebirth comes as falsehoods die,
Amid shattered illusions, futures lie.

In the ruin, strength is found,
In broken pieces, life's resound.
Healing starts, wings spread high,
Beyond shattered illusions, dreams comply.

Canvas of Honesty

Blank slate spread with open heart,
Brushstrokes bold, no place for art.
Colors blend with truth in sight,
On a canvas of honesty, pure and white.

Each layer tells a tale so true,
Every hue a story too.
Transparencies bathe in light,
On this canvas of honesty, take flight.

Mistakes and triumphs side by side,
No need for secrets here to hide.
Realities mixed, wrong and right,
Crafting a canvas of honesty, bright.

Truths unspoken find their place,
Open spaces, no disgrace.
Raw and real, with every night,
On this canvas of honesty, insight.

Completed work, a masterpiece,
Bearing answers, subtle peace.
Wholeness found in purest sight,
From a canvas of honesty, delight.

Secrets Laid Bare

In shadows deep, where whispers lie,
A silent tale doth weave.
Unveiled beneath the moonlit sky,
The heart begins to grieve.

A hidden truth, a dark affair,
With fervor does it cling.
In quiet moments, secrets bare,
Their haunting voices sing.

Ephemeral, the dreams that fade,
Like dew at morning's light.
Yet what in darkness was displayed,
Now dances in our sight.

The heart, once cloaked in mystery,
Now open to the world.
In every secret, history
Like fragile leaves unfurled.

In truth's embrace, we find our way,
Through woven strands of time.
The secrets that have led astray
Become our truthful rhyme.

Undeniable Realities

The sun shall rise, the night shall fall,
The cycle knows no end.
In nature's rhythm, we find all,
The truths we can't pretend.

The river flows with ceaseless grace,
Its path carved through the land.
In every turn, in every pace,
Life's truths we understand.

The seasons change, as do our days,
An undeniable fact.
In every breath, in countless ways,
Time's impact is exact.

Mountains stand, unyielding guards,
Witnesses to our plight.
In their stark, unchanging regards,
We see eternal might.

Reality, a mirrored glass,
Reflects our fleeting dreams.
In its embrace, it lets us pass,
Through life's unfailing streams.

Inner Realms

Within the silent, shadowed place,
Where minds and spirits meet,
A sacred, secret inner space,
Away from daily beat.

In realms of thought and dreams we roam,
Unbridled, wild and free.
A sanctuary, a mental home,
A boundless, deep blue sea.

Here lies the truth, the core of soul,
Untouched by outside lies.
In this internal, private whole,
Our purest self resides.

Through introspection, journeys made,
We navigate our fears.
In inner realms, no light doth fade,
No sorrow soils with tears.

From deep within, the strength is found,
To face the world anew.
For in these realms where thoughts abound,
The spirit's light shines true.

Pure Perception

A world perceived through honest eyes,
Untainted by our fears.
In every sight, a truth implies,
A clarity appears.

Remove the veil of bias keen,
Seek what is pure and clear.
In simple things, the beauty seen,
Unclouded, sincere.

In raindrop's fall and sun's warm hue,
In nature's grand display,
A world of wonders, always true,
Seen in a million ways.

Pure perception, unfiltered view,
Shows life in honest form.
A mirror to a heart that's true,
A shelter in the storm.

Let's cast aside the judgment, false,
Embrace what senses bring.
Through pure perception, life exalts,
In every living thing.

Hidden Lenses

Through lenses veiled, the world does change,
A secret view, within our range.
The colors shift, the shapes may blend,
A hidden truth, around each bend.

We walk on paths no eyes have seen,
In misty gray, and shades between.
Yet clarity awaits the few,
Who see with hearts, a vision true.

Behind the glass, where shadows play,
Lie whispered words we dare not say.
They guide us on, these unseen guides,
Through nights of dark, to brighter tides.

Our eyes may fail, but souls perceive,
The silent truths we can't conceive.
With hidden lenses, clear as dawn,
The world's illusions are withdrawn.

To see, to know, beyond the veil,
Is not a gift that eyes avail.
In every heart, the lens is set,
Unlock the view, and never forget.

Epiphany of Essence

In realms not bound by space or time,
Where thought and soul begin to rhyme.
We find the essence of our kind,
Unknown by sense, but felt by mind.

A spark, a flicker, then a blaze,
Awoken by this mental daze.
An epiphany, so pure, so bright,
Transforming all in its light.

Beyond the veil of common sight,
Lies truth unknown, yet infinite.
Through silent whispers in the air,
We grasp the 'why', the 'how', the 'where'.

Within the stillness, answers bloom,
No longer bound by doubt or gloom.
The essence speaks, in quiet thought,
And wisdom, once elusive, sought.

As stars align within our hearts,
The truth of essence life imparts.
An epiphany, both vast and small,
Reveals our unity with all.

Unmasking All

We wear our masks, from dawn to night,
In patterns dark, or colors bright.
They hide our fears, conceal our pain,
Yet in the shadows, truths remain.

A single tear, a gentle sigh,
Reveals the soul behind the lie.
In moments real, the masks may fall,
And we unmask, revealing all.

With courage drawn from hearts so deep,
We peel the layers, often steep.
To bare ourselves, a daunting task,
Yet liberating from the mask.

In vulnerability, we find,
The strength to leave our chains behind.
Unmasking all, we come to see,
The boundless truth of being free.

For in the end, the masks we wear,
Are barriers to love and care.
Unmasking all, we stand as one,
In open light, beneath the sun.

Secrets Disclosed

In whispered winds, and shadows long,
Lie secrets kept, both right and wrong.
Unknown to all, yet deeply sown,
Within the hearts, of those alone.

A secret told, in hushed lament,
Can shatter walls, or just cement.
Its power lies in what we share,
The truth revealed, beyond compare.

Yet some remain beneath the waves,
In silent depths, like hidden caves.
Awaiting time, or breaking trust,
To rise from ashes, or turn to dust.

With breath withheld, we hold our ground,
In secrets deep, no voice or sound.
But when disclosed, the heart can heal,
And souls, once chained, begin to feel.

The scars, the tales, our secrets bear,
Are woven threads of human care.
In disclosing all, we find release,
And hearts united, rest in peace.

Seeing Beyond

Glimpses of the unseen grace,
Through the webs we often trace,
In the shadows light imbued,
Marvels hidden, yet construed.

Mysteries within the fold,
Stories whispered, rarely told,
Past the veils of mundane sight,
Lies a realm of pure delight.

Colors blend in spectral hue,
Truth emerges, always new,
Every thought a cosmic dance,
Guiding us in silent trance.

Eyes that pierce through time and space,
Find the wonder, seek the place,
Where the heart and spirit lie,
Infinite beneath the sky.

Beyond the realm of simple sight,
Dwells a world, pure and bright,
See it with your soul's embrace,
Life's profound, enchanting face.

Intrinsic Perceptions

Within the essence of the mind,
Lies a beauty, undefined,
Shapes and whispers flow like streams,
Crafting realms of hidden dreams.

Thoughts as feathers gently land,
On the shores of wonderland,
In the silence of the night,
Stars reveal their secret light.

Each reflection, deep and clear,
Holds a truth we hold so dear,
In the depths of introspection,
Life unveils its true direction.

Perceptions shaped by inner flame,
Guide us through this shifting game,
Every sense a thread of gold,
Weaving tales of life untold.

In the quiet, feel the sound,
Find the truths that circle round,
Within the heart, mind, and soul,
Lie the keys to make us whole.

Naked Elegance

In the stillness stripped away,
Lies a truth we dare not sway,
Bare and bold, so pure, so bright,
Morning's first and tender light.

Beauty worn with no disguise,
Reflects in unassuming eyes,
Grace that hums in nature's tune,
Underneath the silver moon.

Simple form of gentle sway,
In the night and in the day,
Elegance in lines so fine,
Patterned by a grand design.

Stripped of all the worldly guise,
Pure as tears from empty skies,
Naked in its endless grace,
Lies the soul's most gentle place.

In true form, without a mask,
Lives the soul's transcendent task,
To reflect the core divine,
Through each silent, sacred line.

Uncovered Whispers

In the night's embrace we lie,
Whispers fading, by and by,
Secrets shared on breeze so light,
Veiled in shadow, out of sight.

Words unspoken, soft and low,
In the silence, tendrils grow,
Echoes of a distant song,
Fading not, but ever strong.

Hidden tales in whispers wrought,
Stories sewn in webs of thought,
In the heart, their beat remains,
Through the joys and through the pains.

Whispers of the world at night,
Hold the truths we seek in light,
Touch the soul with gentle grace,
Leave behind a silent trace.

Listen closely, hear the sound,
Secrets float and swirl around,
In uncovered whispers' dance,
Lies our soul's most true romance.

Reality Laid Bare

In shadows deep, the world does lie,
A veil of dreams masks every sigh.
Yet truths unfold as dawn breaks bare,
Revealing all that lingers there.

The morning light doth gently play,
Unveiling secrets of the day.
In quiet corners, far from gleam,
Reality, a lucid dream.

Whispers soft in twilight's brew,
Call forth the heart, the soul to view.
In moments vast, where time stands still,
The essence of existence will.

Through veils and mists, illusions fall,
Unmasked, we see the truth of all.
With open eyes, the world laid bare,
A tapestry beyond compare.

Embrace the light, let shadows fade,
In clarity, the truth is made.
The lines of life, both light and dark,
Compose the song, a vital spark.

Ethereal Truths

In realms of mist, where whispers flow,
The ethereal truths begin to show.
Beyond the sight of mundane eyes,
Eternal secrets softly rise.

The stars, they speak in cryptic glow,
Of why the winds of fate do blow.
In cosmic dance, the truths align,
We glimpse what lies beyond the line.

In fleeting dreams and quiet dawns,
The veil of glass, it dulls, then wanes.
We touch the fabric of the soul,
And know the depths, the whole, the whole.

Among the waves, within the breeze,
Lie answers to life's mysteries.
In moments still, and hearts so pure,
The ethereal truths endure.

Embrace the unknown, cherish the dark,
In twilight's realm, our spirits hark.
The paths we walk, the lives we lead,
Are whispered truths our hearts can read.

Undisguised Realms

Within the quiet of the night,
The undisguised realms come to light.
In dreams uncaged and thoughts so clear,
The hidden truths, they soon appear.

The masks we wear, they fall away,
Revealing what our souls convey.
In every breath, a silver line,
Connecting all, the grand design.

Through crystal streams, in forest deep,
The realms of truth are ours to seek.
In nature's mirth, and starlit skies,
The undisguised, before us lies.

The boundaries fade, the walls dissolve,
Our spirits rise, our hearts involve.
We see the world, as it is meant,
A place of peace and pure content.

Let go of fear, and open wide,
The realms are here, for none to hide.
In every heart, the truth does dwell,
An undisguised, enchanting spell.

The Heart of Matter

Beneath the layers, masks and guise,
The heart of matter gently lies.
A core of truth, so bright and warm,
Within the calm, amidst the storm.

In sacred space, where silence reigns,
The essence pure, it yet remains.
In every soul, the spark is found,
Connecting all, unbound, unbound.

Through trials faced and tears endured,
Our hearts reveal what is assured.
In every beat, a rhythm true,
The heart of matter comes to view.

No walls can hold, no shadows veil,
The light within that shall prevail.
In unity, in love, we find,
The heart of matter intertwined.

So seek the depths, embrace the whole,
In every part, a kindred soul.
The heart of matter, simple, clear,
Is all we need, forever near.

Confessions of Existence

Beneath the shroud of star-kissed dreams,
A whisper carries fragile schemes.
In shadows cast by lunar beams,
Our hearts unveil their hidden themes.

The silent echoes of our past,
Through forests deep, they wander fast.
Life's currents sweep, our truths unmasked,
In twilight's glow, our fears contrast.

A tapestry of souls entwined,
Within the cosmos, intertwined.
In sacred bonds, our thoughts confined,
In whispered truths, our hearts aligned.

The sands of time in steady flow,
With every grain, our secrets grow.
In hearts of dusk, we come to know,
The whispered truths, the ebb and flow.

In moments caught between the stars,
We find ourselves in earthly scars.
Through whispered night, in lunar bars,
We face our truth, no longer far.

The Essence Exposed

In the quiet dawn's embrace,
A fleeting glimpse of heaven's grace.
We find ourselves, in nature's pace,
Our souls laid bare, our true face.

The wind, a gentle, silent guide,
Through valleys deep, it does confide.
In whispered tones, it speaks inside,
Exposing truths that we can't hide.

The river's song, a soothing sound,
In every drop, our love is found.
Through winding paths, it wraps around,
Our hearts revealed, no longer bound.

The mountains stand in silent might,
Their peaks a testament of light.
In shadows cast from day to night,
We see our essence, clear as sight.

In nature's realm, our spirits soar,
Our inner truths we can't ignore.
With every step, we find much more,
Our essence, pure, in nature's core.

Raw Epiphanies

In moments hushed, the mind takes flight,
A spark ignites, revealing night.
In shadows deep, a fierce insight,
The truth emerges, pure and bright.

A whisper soft, an inner call,
Through silent halls, it crescendos tall.
In quiet thoughts, we break the wall,
Our raw epiphanies enthrall.

The heart, a drum, it beats anew,
In every throb, our fears accrue.
In voices born of midnight hue,
Our secret selves we come to view.

A mirror clear, it shows the way,
Reflections caught in light of day.
In truths we hide, we go astray,
Yet in epiphanies, we lay.

With every dawn, a chance to see,
The depths of our complexity.
In raw epiphanies, we're free,
To be our truest, verily.

Mirrors of Reality

In the silence of the morning's breath,
We face the truths unspoken yet.
Through mirrors wrought in nature's depth,
Our souls reflect without regret.

The glass of time, it does not lie,
In every shard, our stories sigh.
We see our lives, as they pass by,
In mirrors of reality's eye.

Each moment caught in crystal clear,
A glimpse of truth, a tethered tear.
In mirrors held so close, so near,
Our hidden fears do reappear.

Through looking glass, our hearts revealed,
In every glance, our wounds are healed.
In mirrors, truth cannot be sealed,
Reality's touch, our fate is sealed.

In reflections deep, we come to know,
The parts of us we seldom show.
Through mirrors wide, our spirits grow,
In reality's light, our truths bestow.